Jesus The Indescribable Gift:
Devotions and Meditations 2014

Jesus The Indescribable Gift: Devotions and Meditations

Jesus The Indescribable Gift
Devotions and Meditations 2014

By

Members of Main Line Black Interdenominational Ministers Alliance

Rev. Dr. Marsha Brown Woodard
Editor-in-Chief

Jesus The Indescribable Gift
Devotions and Meditations 2014
Edited by Rev. Dr. Marsha Brown Woodard

© 2014 Main Line Black Interdenominational Alliance

Publisher: brown bridges press
ISBN: 978-1889819419

Greetings

Grace and peace be multiplied unto each of you!

In these pages the members of the Main Line Black Interdenominational Ministers Alliance share about the very best gift ever received: Jesus Christ. We share this Devotional as our gift to you and we hope that you are eager to begin to unwrap it, so that you can see all that is inside.

I am sure that all of you have received a variety of gifts in your life time. Some I imagined have been so beautifully wrapped that you almost didn't want to take the wrapping off! Yet, you knew that unless you did you would never get to the real gift that was inside.

Likewise we hope that these devotionals, wrapped in the pages of this book, will be one of those gifts that once the wrapping has been removed will help you get to the real gift, the very best gift of all: Jesus.

So open the book. Read it. Be guided by the words and the scriptures. Unwrap the package and experience the gift.

We also hope the book will be a tool that God uses to strengthen your relationship with Him, and that it helps you to grow as a follower of Christ.

Jesus is the greatest gift that the world has ever received! Each of us thank God for sending us the best gift ever, Jesus the Christ. And we hope you, as you read this book, will be even more committed to serving God with all your heart mind and soul than ever before.

In His Service
Rev. Albert Johnson
President, MLBIMA

Contributors

Rev Paul Adkins

Rev. Carlos Bounds

Rev. Darrell Brown, Jr.

Rev. Albert G. Davis, Jr.

Rev. Scott Dorsey

Minister Eileen Evans

Minister Jeannette Myers-Gilbert

Rev. Rashad Groves

Minister Carlton Hatcher

Minister Manuel Howard

Rev. Albert Johnson

Rev. April Martin

Rev. Joell D. McDuffy

Elder Darren Miller

Rev. Lawrence Pannell

Rev. James Pollard, Sr. PhD

Rev. Michael Stitt

Rev. Dr. Marsha Brown Woodard

Table of Contents

Contributors iii

Table of Contents v

Let The Unwrapping Start!! 1

Jesus Christ, The Good & Perfect Gift from God!! 3

The Gift That Never Fades Nor Decays 5

The Gift of a Son 7

I Got It! 12

God Is Love 15

Unity 17

Friends and Friendship as 19

Gifts That Keep on Giving 19

Actions Speak Louder than Words 21

The Gift That Keeps On Giving 25

A Divine Intervention 28

Thank You for the Indescribable Gift 31

Trusting God 33

A Witness For Jesus! 35

The Total Package 38

It Is All About Trust 41

Obedience is Better than Sacrifice 43

The Gift of Eternal Life 45

Absolutely Indescribable 9

An Encounter with Jesus 49

The Weaving of Our Lives Together 52

Let The Unwrapping Start!!

Gifts are wonderful to receive. Many times they come wrapped in beautiful paper but no matter how beautiful the wrapping may be it is not the real gift. We have to unwrap it for the real gift is inside.

This book is our gift to you and we hope that even though the cover is beautiful that you can't wait to get inside! The members of the Mainline Black Interdenominational Ministers Alliance know that Jesus is the best gift of all, and each meditation has been written to help you know a little more about this gift. As you turn the pages and begin to unwrap this gift you will discover that you have actually been given multiple gifts, for each devotional is a gift that has come from their hearts with love.

As you read this book we pray that you will receive insights and will see even more what an indescribable gift Jesus really is.

As you read we encourage you to listen for the voice of God and when you hear God speak, take a Selah moment: time to pause and think about what you have read. As you read and as you hear from God we hope that it will inspire you to add your own thoughts. So, write in this book, mark it up, and make it yours.

1

Most of all we hope that as you hear from God through these pages you will be more committed than ever to serving God with all your heart, mind and soul and you will be led to share the greatest gift of all with every one you meet.

We thank God for sending us the best gift ever, his only begotten son, Jesus, who has become our Savior.

Jesus Christ, The Good & Perfect Gift from God!!

Minister Manuel A. Howard, M.Div.
Bethel Bryn Mawr A.M.E. Church, Bryn Mawr, PA

"Every good and perfect gift is from above, coming down from the father of the heavenly lights, who does not change like shifting shadows. James 1:17 (NIV)

Have you ever seen something so beautiful that words could not describe the action, sound, voice, moment, or image? James chapter 1 in verse 17 says it best. "Every good and perfect gift is from above, coming down from the father of the heavenly lights, who does not change like shifting shadows."

Jesus, the perfect indescribable gift, redeemed us from sin and death. This indescribable gift opened the only doorway leading to eternal life in heaven with God the father.

This indescribable gift died on the cross bearing excruciating pain and in 3 days rose from the dead to ascend into heaven to assume his rightful position at the right hand of God the father.

This indescribable gift, Jesus, left the Holy Spirit for our comfort, our protection, our guidance, and our power in Christ Jesus.

This indescribable gift was given to us by God the father because of his great love and amazing grace. "For God so loved the world that whoever believes in Him shall not perish but have everlasting life. For God did not send His son into the world to condemn the world but to save the world through him."

Jesus Christ the indescribable gift. Trust in Him, seek Him, find Him, try Him and follow Him!

This indescribable gift, Jesus, will transform your mind, body, soul, and life into eternity. If he did it for me, He will do it for you. God is just waiting for you to open your heart, soul, and mind to receive the indescribable gift He gave with all His heart!!

Amen, Amen, and Amen

The Gift That Never Fades Nor Decays

Rev. Paul Clifford Adkins, Presiding Elder Retired
Bethel AME Church, Bryn Mawr, PA

"Thanks be to God for his unspeakable Gift." 2 Cor. 9:15

When I was a child I looked so to Christmas because I knew I would be receiving gifts. It did not mean I would be receiving gifts because I had been so good; it was because my mother and father loved me so. Sure, I had not always been the best child and had run afoul of their rules; they let me know this by my punishments. But they loved me in spite of my faults.

I was always so happy for the gifts I received for my birthday as well. But these gifts did not last long. Sure I played with the toys and games and I wore the clothes. But the games and toys faded after the luster wore off. The clothes were soon outgrown and laid aside. And so it is with material things, they soon fade away and decay.

But I would like to explain what a gift is. It is that which is given or bestowed on a person. A gift is anything which is voluntarily transferred by one person to another without compensation. When we accept Christ as our Lord and Savior we receive an indescribable gift from

God. For God so loved the world that he gave his only begotten Son, that whosoever believeth in him should not perish, but have everlasting life. (John 3:16).

This gift was given not because we have been so good, not because we have all ways kept God's law, not because we joined the church. No, it is because God loved us so that he gave us Jesus the Indescribable Gift.

An indescribable gift is one that cannot be described; it is beyond the power of description. It is beyond our comprehension to understand the love of God that He would send his only beloved son as an offering for the world. "For the wages of sin is death but the gift of God is eternal life through Jesus Christ our Lord." (Ro. 6:23)

It is ours to except or reject this gift of love. If we accept it we will live in God's presence through eternity. If not, we will be cast into outer darkness separated from God for ever.

The Gift of a Son

James A Pollard Sr. PhD, Pastor
Zion Baptist Church, Ardmore PA

"For a child will be born to us, a son will be given to us; ..."
Isaiah 9:6a (NAST)

This passage of scripture speaks to us in terms of what has been given to us by the Lord, a *son*. In our cultural context being told a son will be given to us is trite. But in the time of Isaiah, this announcement was special.

The announcement of a son being born meant:

1. The family name would be continued
2. The parents (especially the women) had financial security, and
3. They, (the entire family) would have protection

Isn't it wonderful how Lord, by his death and resurrection, provided the same things to all who believe on Him? As Christians we are now the sons and daughters (heirs) of God (Galatians 4:7 NAST).

Therefore we are given by God, through Jesus, financial security. "God shall supply all our needs..." (Philippians

4:19 NAST) We are the heirs of God so His name will be continued and finally, God will protect us (Isaiah 31:5 NAST).

Thank you God for the gift of your son Jesus, our life, our security our protector. We love you Lord, and we are grateful for your gift: a son!

Absolutely Indescribable

Reverend Carlos D. Bounds, Pastor
Bethel AME Church, Bryn Mawr, PA

Thanks be to God for his indescribable gift!
2 Corinthians 9:15 (NIV)

I have received some gifts in my life that have been too extraordinary to describe … sometimes in good ways and sometimes in challenging situations.

Indescribable is defined as not describable or too extraordinary for description. So like I stated before I have received gifts that have been too extraordinary to describe both good and challenging. However, in describing our God and his gifts we will never be disappointed but only blessed and satisfied.

Some gifts we receive from the world can only serve for one purpose, such as a sweater for the season, or some other object for a particular purpose. God's gift of Christ Jesus is a gift that is indescribable.

When we observe Christ Jesus it is remarkable of what we have in him as a gift. Number one he is the Savior of the entire world. There is nothing in all the world that could

9

have done for us what God did through Jesus Christ. What gift could be compared with the gift of God's son who gave up his life so that we could live eternally with him?

The scripture says "while we are yet sinners Christ died for us." (Romans 5:8) This is a description of what an indescribable gift is: something that is too extraordinary to describe. The scripture also says "for ye know the grace of our Lord Jesus Christ, that though he was rich became poor, that ye through his poverty might be rich." (2 Corinthians 8:9) This again describes that Jesus Christ is an indescribable gift.

We now know that Jesus is not only a Savior but he is also a healer. The bible declares that he was "wounded for our transgression bruised for our iniquities: the chastisement of our peace was upon; and with his stripes we are healed." (Isaiah 53:5)

Once again, here is a gift that is able to do more than one thing and is able to save and heal at the same time. This is absolutely indescribable knowing that our gift from God is not describable but too extraordinary for description.

We also know that God is a provider because the scripture also says that "our God will supply all your

need according to his riches in glory by Christ Jesus."
(Philippians 4:19)

Finally, nothing in all the world can give us a gift that can
save, heal, and provide. However, the gift of God in Jesus
Christ can do even more than this because the scripture
records the gift saying that "the Spirit of the Lord is upon
me, because he hath anointed me to preach the gospel to
the poor; he hath sent me to heal the brokenhearted, to
preach deliverance to the captives, and recovering of
sight to the blind, to set at liberty them that are bruised, to
preach the acceptable year of the Lord." (Luke 4:18)

We ought to praise God for the indescribable gift that is
able to do "exceedingly and abundantly above all that we
ask or think, according to the power that worketh in us."
(Ephesians 3:20)

I Got It!

Elder Darren Miller, Pastor
Memorial Church of God in Christ - Haverford, PA

"Thanks be unto God for his unspeakable gift."
2 Corinthians 9:15 (KJV)

Jesus – the greatest gift that was ever given.
Jesus – the greatest love that could ever be shown.

As a child one of my greatest memories of happy anticipation was knowing that a special day was approaching. Sometimes it was the anticipation of my birthday, but unequivocally, the anticipation of Christmas Day was at the top of the list.

There was always something about Christmastime that caused other days to look smaller by comparison. As the Christmas season approached, the anticipation of the coming of Christmas seemed to make its coming take even longer.

TV shows were playing Christmas episodes (on all 4 channels that we had, 7 if UHF decided to work that day), TV commercials were advertising new toys. And what could parallel the big catalogues that would come from the department stores in the mail? We would go straight to the toy section and begin marking off what we anticipated getting on Christmas Day without looking or even caring about the cost. We were excited!

The anticipation of receiving the gifts asked for, and hoped for, would cause a child that would otherwise sleep for untold hours on a school day if not awakened, to sleep for only a couple of hours on Christmas Eve, and then wake up out of sheer excitement.

Then came the moment of truth. Emerging from my bedroom in footy-pajamas it was time to go into the living room and see what was under the tree.

Oh what a time of joy and bliss to see the gift that I had received! "I got it!" Possessing that gift was indescribable! Whether it was action figures, a remote control car, a board game, or a new bike, the gift received gave countless hours of fun, and a heart of thankfulness and gratitude.

God's people were in great anticipation of the Messiah, a King, a Ruler, who would deliver them from the oppression they knew at that time. Many had prophesied of His coming, but like Christmas Day, it seemed as if He would never come.

The Bible tells us in Galatians 4: 4-5 (NLT) "[4] But when the right time came, God sent his Son, born of a woman, subject to the law. [5] God sent him to buy freedom for us who were slaves to the law, so that he could adopt us as his very own children."

They had gone into the catalogue and circled what it was they wanted to have for their very own, but the gift that they received was bigger and better than they could have ever anticipated. While they were looking for someone to come in with military might and strong-arm their enemies into subjection, Jesus, the Greatest Gift, the Gift of Love in Person was given not to bring all into condemnation, but to bring eternal life.

John 3: 16-17 (NLT) declares [16] "For God loved the world so much that he gave his one and only Son, so that everyone who believes in him will not perish but have eternal life. [17] God sent his Son into the world not to judge the world, but to save the world through him.

The excitement of receiving the Gift must remain within us today. As we invite those who have not received the free Gift, Jesus Christ, to experience the love that He gave us, the anticipation is that they too will receive this wonderful, indescribable Gift given so that we might receive.

God Is Love

Rev. Darrell C. Brown Jr., Pastor
New Hope Baptist Church, Paoli, PA

> *...Beloved, if God so loved us, we also ought to love one another. No one has seen God at any time; if we love one another, God abides in us, and His love is perfected in us. By this we know that we abide in Him and He in us, because He has given us of His Spirit. 1 John 4:11-13*

"Love recognizes no barriers. It jumps hurdles, leaps fences, penetrates walls to arrive at it destination full of hope." (Maya Angelou)

Love is an action word. Love is never content to simply exist, it must act. In fact, love usually proves itself by what it does. No matter what someone says, it is often very difficult for us to believe that they love us if they never demonstrate their love.

God loves us and has acted on that love. Scripture teaches us that "God demonstrated his love towards us that while we were yet sinners Christ died for us" (Romans 5:8).

Think about it, God did not wait for us to love him, or wait for us to be good; but when we were unloving, and not doing the right things God showed us how much he loved us. Like the quote from Maya Angelou, God showed us what love looks like when it removes barriers.

God sent his only begotten son for the whole world. Whoever believes is welcomed into God's family. We can take comfort as Christians in the fact that the God we serve has acted in love and has proven his love to us by sending his son, Jesus, and if we believe in him we will not perish but we will have everlasting life. (John 3:16 paraphrase)

Unity

Rev. Lawrence C. Pannell, Associate Minister
Second Baptist Church, Wayne, PA

"How Good and how pleasant it is for brethren to dwell together in unity" Psalm 133:1-3 (KJV)

Unity is a word used to signify the oneness of sentiment, affection or behavior that should exist among the people of God. There are many places in scripture that speak of this unity but let me share a few here.

In Psalm 133:1 we find, "Behold how good and pleasant it is for brethren (sisters) to dwell together in Unity". The Psalmist seems to say that when the people of God are able to exist in unity the outcome is good and the atmosphere is pleasant.

In Ephesians 4:13 we read about the unity that comes through faith and belief in the same great truths of God. Paul writing to the church at Ephesus encouraged them to "... walked in the light as he (Jesus) is in the light we have fellowship one with another which is "Unity".

For guidance to work together in "Unity" read Eph. 4:1-13.

For guidance to pray together in "Unity" read Matt.18:19-20.

And let us not grow weary while doing good, endure to keep the "Unity" as we all come in the "Unity" of faith. Always remember we cannot have Unity without "U" in it.

Friends and Friendship as Gifts That Keep on Giving

Minister Eileen Evans, Associate Minister
Mt. Calvary Baptist Church, Ardmore, PA

"Every time I think of you, I give thanks to my God."
Philippians 1:3 (NLT)

The Apostle Paul is known as much for his deep theology and corrective letters as for his studied life and life of servanthood to the Lord Jesus Christ. He is known for his highs and lows in ministry (see II Cor. 4: 7-10) and in this passage he was writing to the 'Believers' at Philippi who had demonstrated themselves to be true friends. Paul knew that it was a gift to have true friends. True friends are friends of the heart…people who are more concerned about your character than about your comfort.

Recently, I received a card. The relevant sentiments are as follows:
"You are my friend when I am glad,
You are my crutch when times are bad.
You are my shoulder when I am sad,
You are my reasoning when I am mad.
Yet, you always know when to let me be…"

The card is one that I will treasure for it was a gift to have someone see me as this kind of friend.

True friendship and fellowship is spiritual and is a gift from God (every good and perfect is from above – James 1:17). Not that the people are perfect (for certainly neither of us are either perfect or necessarily good), but the gift of friendship is a good and perfect gift.

So, even in the midst of Paul's struggling, he could think of the multi-faceted kindnesses of his friends at Philippi and utter a prayer of thanksgiving every time he thought of them. Paul challenges us to think of kindness we have received from friends.

Thank You Lord for the gifts of friends and friendship. Thank You even more that these friends and friendships are designed to mimic the friendship and fellowship You desire to share with us.

Actions Speak Louder than Words

Minister Carlton B. Hatcher, Assistant Pastor
Youth Ministries, Zion Baptist Church, Ardmore, PA

"Thanks be to God for His Indescribable Gift"
2 Corinthians 9:15 NIV

I overheard a conversation the other day between two of my co-workers. One was sharing with the other, the frustration he has with people who give him clothes as gifts even though he has asked them repeatedly not to do so. He said that they are usually the wrong size, the wrong color, the wrong style and usually when he goes to return them there is always some kind of problem.

This is a situation I'm sure that we're all familiar with. But nothing could be further from the truth when we speak of the indescribable "gift of God" Jesus Christ.

Jesus is the one who Pilate said, "In him I can find no fault" (Luke 23:4) and the one the Bible asks the question, "Is there anything too hard for the Lord" (Gen. 18:14)? So in our gift there is no wrong and he is a "problem solver."

We've all gotten gifts for our birthday, a special holiday or a special occasion and those who were unable to take part in the celebration will always ask us, "What did you get?" Then we begin to describe the various gifts that we got so that those who weren't there might share in the joy of the celebration as well.

Well, thanks be to God that one day over 2000 years ago God couldn't watch us "self destruct" anymore. So, because he's loving, compassionate, gracious and merciful, God gave us his only Son, Jesus Christ the most precious and indescribable gift of all.

Yes indescribable. Let's face it:

- How could we even begin to try to describe his **authority**. The disciples asked the question one day, "What manner of man is this, that even the winds and the waves obey him" (Mk 4:41)?
- And what about his **miraculous works**, "Then he took the five loaves and two fishes..." (Luke 9:16) and fed five thousand men beside the women and children.
- And what about his **bedside manner,** when he says to the paralytic, "Arise, and take up your bed, and walk" (Mk 2:9)

- And what about his **acts of restoration** when he said to the woman, "I Am the Resurrection and the life, he that believeth in me, though he were dead, yet shall he live:" (John 11:25)
- How can one begin to try to describe his **omnipotence** when said, "I Am Alpha and Omega" (Rev.1:8)

This indescribable gift of God that we have received came to save us from our sin and that in and of itself is a most memorable celebratory day.

For those who weren't a part of that celebration and ask the question, "What is this joy that you have?" we must make every effort to share the "gospel of Jesus Christ." We must convey his many virtues (agape, joy, peace, patience, gentleness, goodness, faith, meekness and self-control) so that those we encounter along the way would come to know him as we do, so that we might all celebrate Jesus together and experience "abundant and eternal life" through the joy of our salvation.

The Gift That Keeps On Giving

Reverend Albert G. Davis, Jr., Pastor
Mt. Calvary Baptist Church, Ardmore, PA

"On the last day, that great day of the feast, Jesus stood and cried out, saying, "If anyone thirsts, let him come to Me and drink. He who believes in Me, as the Scripture has said, out of his heart will flow rivers of living water." But this He spoke concerning the Spirit, whom those believing in Him would receive; for the Holy Spirit was not yet given, because Jesus was not yet glorified." John 7:37-39 (NKJV)

The "gift that keeps on giving" was popularized as a catchphrase, and widely known and used as a marketing slogan for the phonograph circa 1924. Since that time, many other commercials have touted this phrase as an incentive to purchase their products.

According to *Your Dictionary*, an on-line resource, "The 'gift that keeps on giving' is meant to invoke the feelings people get when they receive a present. Any present that gives that feeling over and over, such as receiving a magazine every month, would be better than a gift that only provides that feeling once." Any repeat gift, that evokes the same sentiments over and over again or a one-time gift that seems to have lasting and recurrent after effects would qualify as a "gift that keeps on giving."

But Jesus said it best when He spoke of rivers of living water. Although He mentioned "living waters" to the Samaritan woman at the well (John 4), its meaning super abounds to all Believers.

In our key scripture, Jesus once again speaks of this on-going gift when He says "rivers of living water will flow from within". Note, He said, "rivers" (plural)…not river (singular); not stream, not pond, not fountain…but **rivers** of living water. Note again, it is **living** water…not stagnant, placid, or dead. Not even calm, cool and collected, but living waters. Living implies life, health, sustenance, and growth.

Jesus said this referring to the Holy Spirit – the indwelling, continuous presence of the abiding Spirit of God. The imagery is magnificent; like a continuously flowing river tumbling from mountain peaks to valley river beds. The Holy Spirit who is able to meet us anywhere on this life's journey – whether we are having a mountain top experience or trekking through the valley… His abiding presence is with us.

Can you imagine the continuous flow and flowing of the indwelling Spirit of God? We experience His presence, flowing through Believers, rising up to meet all of our needs and many of our wants. We experience His presence, not as a one and done event, but constantly. We experience His presence, not only as a personal blessing but as a means of blessings to others.

In essence, we become a blessed channel of blessings (rivers of living waters) so that all whose path we cross can experience the life giving flow of the gift that keeps on giving.

Praise God from whom all blessings flow!

A Divine Intervention

Rev. Joell D. McDuffy, Pastor
St. John A.M.E. Church, Wayne, PA

But now that you've found you don't have to listen to sin tell you what to do, and have discovered the delight of listening to God telling you, what a surprise! A whole, healed, put-together life right now, with more and more of life on the way! Work hard for sin your whole life and your pension is death. But God's gift is real life, eternal life, delivered by Jesus, our Master. Romans 6:22-23, The Message Bible.

There is a very interesting show on the A&E Network called *Intervention* in which viewers are able to watch a person suffering from drug and alcohol addiction self-destruct before their eyes. The show chronicles the struggles of the subject who is in danger of dying as a result of their addiction. A group of loved ones plan and execute an intervention. They, along with professional addiction counselors, confront the subject about their addiction.

During the intervention, the subject is given an ultimatum – either go into a rehabilitation center immediately or face the possibility of losing contact with loved ones, custody of their children and ultimately their lives. The subject must decide if he/she is willing to accept the help that has been offered and enter rehab or continue down the same destructive path.

Truth be told, all of us were in need of an intervention. We were headed for hell. Our lives were steeped in sin and we were looking for love and satisfaction in all the wrong places. We were chasing the next high of a new car, a better job, more money, fame, sex or success. What we found was temporary joy and fleeting satisfaction and when we came down from that high, we found that the emptiness was still there.

God knew that humankind was in trouble, that people would be sentenced to spiritual death because of sin. God decided to initiate a divine intervention on our behalf.

God's intervention did not involve rehab. God's intervention involved a gift, the gift of salvation, the gift of forgiveness of sins, and the gift of an abundant life. This gift was given in the life of God's only begotten son, Jesus the Christ. John 3:16 says, "For God so loved the world that he gave his only begotten Son, that whosoever believes in him shall not perish, but have everlasting life."

God's intervention does not involve ultimatums. God gives us freewill and a choice to either accept Jesus as our

Savior and live ... or continue down the same path which leads to physical and spiritual death.

The resurrection is the culmination of a divine intervention on our behalf. If you have never accepted Christ, you are the subject. Will you accept or reject God's divine intervention?

Thank You for the Indescribable Gift

Minister Eileen Evans, Associate Minister
Mt. Calvary Baptist Church, Ardmore, PA

Now thanks be to God for His Gift, [precious] beyond telling
[His indescribable, inexpressible, free Gift]!
II Cor. 9:15 (Amplified)

Have you ever been "wow-ed"? Utterly blown away,
moved to tears but left speechless by someone else's
actions or words towards you?

Was the kindness so kind, was the generosity so
generous, or was the graciousness so gracefully offered
you couldn't find adequate words? Was the entire
experience so unexpectedly benevolent that you were
reduced to such an emotional mess that at that moment
you were only able to mutter a barely audible "thank
you?"

Well, if earthly things/people/gifts can elicit such a
response, how much more should we fall at His feet in
total admiration, adoration, worship and praise?

While we were yet sinners – outright and proclaimed
enemies of God – God gave His Only Begotten Son –

offering us not only the gift of salvation but the gift of His Son, Jesus the Christ…a double portion of what we can't really, accurately or adequately describe. O, I think I have found the right word: Indescribable!

We have a tendency to place great weight on temporal things and feather weight to spiritual matters. As grateful as I am for all of my blessings, I have decided to recognize the weightiness of the spiritual blessings. So, I ask you again, "Have you ever been wow-ed?"

Dear Lord…with all that I am, I appreciate your loving kindness towards me. At a loss for multiple words, I simply say, with a grateful heart, "Thank You."

Trusting God

Rev. Michael Stitt, Pastor
Saints Memorial Baptist Church, Bryn Mawr, PA

"Trust in the Lord with all your heart and lean not to your own understanding; in all your ways acknowledge Him and He shall direct our Paths" (Proverbs 3:5-6)

We live in a time where there seems to be so much distrust. There is distrust between countries, governments, churches, families and people in general. Being surrounded with so much distrust we often aren't sure if there is anyone who is worthy of our trust.

Fortunately, during these times of uncertainty, we can always Trust God.

There are many places in scripture that talk about trust. I like Proverbs 3: 5-6 that tells us to "Trust in the Lord with all your heart and lean not to your own understanding; in all your ways acknowledge Him and He shall direct our Paths." Learning to trust God leads us to receiving God's gift of direction.

To ensure that we are moving in the right direction in life, we need to consult God. We need to follow Him because He knows where we ought to be and is the only one that can get us there. God is someone that we can rely and depend upon. God will not disappoint us.

As we grow in trust, we will be able to bring our concerns and needs to God. Regardless of the situation or circumstance we can give all things to God. Scripture calls this committing, so we want to commit all things to God.

Another passage that I like is Psalm 37:5 that states, "Commit your way unto the Lord; Trust also in Him and He shall bring it to pass." We need to Commit to God and then Trust God with our:

- Families
- Education
- Careers
- Health
- Ministries
- Church
- Finances
- Communities
- Children
- Lives
- Everything

God can be trusted. When we trust, it is an indication that we are relying on someone other than ourselves. Let's move to committing everything to God and then trusting God with all our hearts. If we do we will experience God directing our paths.

A Witness For Jesus!

Reverend Scott Dorsey, Pastor
Mt. Zion Holmesburg Baptist Church, Philadelphia, PA

"But you shall receive power, the Holy Spirit coming upon you. And you shall be witnesses to Me both in Jerusalem and in all Judea, and in Samaria, and to the end of the earth." Acts1:8

Once we have received the gift of Christ we have work to do, we are called to share the gift with others.

Today we have many ways to tell the story. We have Twitter, Facebook, and Instagram to spread the Gospel. We can use our cell phones or send a text or email. We can still mail a letter or make a visit. However it is done, we must share the gift.

1. As a disciple of Jesus Christ we have a responsibility to use the gifts that God has given us. The Lord puts us in certain positions to be used as an instrument for Jesus. God will provide the power and wisdom of the Holy Spirit to help each of us to make our family, friends, neighbors, enemies transform into fellow disciples.

2. As a disciple of Christ we follow Christ teachings. Those teaching instruct us to make disciples and not

members. Jesus never instructed us to make members, but disciples. We are to follow and walk in the way of Jesus.

3. As we walk and witness for Christ we must live a Christ-like life. When people see you do they see Jesus? Does your life reflect God's teachings? You should not have to open your mouth for people to see the spirit of God in you. God's spirit should be in your talk and in the way you conduct your life. In order for people to respect what you say, they have to see it in your walk. A witness for God can't be walking like the devil. It will confuse people. As a witness of God your life should speak for itself.

4. Witnessing about God is a serious task that we should not take lightly. We need to be prayerful and fully devoted studying the Word of God. We will face challenges and demonic road blocks that will try to stop us from doing God's will. We must be prepared to spread the word of God. Prayer and devotion to God's word helps us be strong in witnessing for The Lord.

5. God wants you. Yes you! He wants you tell somebody about Jesus and what he has done for you. Everyone has something to offer. Don't be afraid of your past. He brought you through it to live and tell the story of how

God has changed your life. Tell someone today how you have been saved from sin and condemnation.

6. Christ gives you the method that you are to follow in your witnessing and in spread of the gospel. You are to witness where you are. Tell somebody about God in your family or your neighborhood. Don't be ashamed to go out in the world and tell a stranger why God is so great.

Today be not afraid to share a scripture or prayer, to share the gift of new life in Christ with others. It may change or save someone's life.

.

The Total Package

Rev. Rashad Groves
First Baptist Church, Wayne, PA

[18] *"The Spirit of the Lord is upon me, because he has anointed me to bring good news to the poor. He has sent me to proclaim release to the captives and recovery of sight to the blind, to let the oppressed go free,* [19] *to proclaim the year of the Lord's favor." Luke 4:18-19*

It was the year of our Lord nineteen hundred and eighty nine and every 7 year old including me wanted a Nintendo game system. Before there was a Play Station, before there was an Xbox, but after the invention of the Atari 2600, the hottest game system money could buy was the Nintendo game system.

The Nintendo came with two games for your video game playing pleasure. One was Mario Brothers and the other was Duck Hunt. I decided that Christmas season that I didn't want a GI Joe. I didn't want any Transformers, He-Man paraphernalia, or Thundercats action figures. All I wanted for Christmas was a Nintendo!

Finally Christmas came around and I was tremendously blessed to have a lot of gifts. They were wrapped so wonderfully, festively, and beautifully on the outside; I just knew my Nintendo had to be on the inside. After opening everything I was extremely sad to discover that I did not get my Nintendo. I was disillusioned, disenchanted, and dismayed.

But there was one more gift to be opened. This gift was wrapped in newspaper. This gift didn't look as good as the other gifts and because this gift did not look as good on the outside I knew there was no way that what I wanted could possibly be on the inside.

After I decided to open it, inside of the newspaper wrapped gift box was my Nintendo. I learned a valuable lesson that day. Sometimes outward appearances can cause us to miss out on the potential and possibilities of what could be on the inside. If we are overly concerned with the package we run the risk of neglecting the promise.

Even our Lord and Liberator Jesus of Nazareth did not arrive in the best package. Born to an unwed single mother, in a manger, in a patriarchal society wasn't the best package. But the gift is greater than the package!

In Luke 4:18-19 when Jesus took the sacred scroll and began to expound, the congregation was filled with anticipation. Jesus was explaining that His advocacy would be specifically on behalf of the poor, the captive, the blind, and the oppressed. Then Jesus wrapped His gift of justice, love, and equality, in a package that His audience had a difficult time accepting.

This gift that Jesus came to offer was not just for Jews but for all humanity. This caused the audience to want to destroy him.

Anytime one has a gift and has the anointed audacity to speak truth to power, to challenge the status quo, to be a voice for the voiceless, you are automatically eligible for danger. That is the cost of a gift. But be encouraged because the great philosopher Niccolò Machiavelli said, "Nothing great is accomplished without *danger."*

Womanist scholar Emilie Townes once said, "A self made person is a bad architecture." I understand that to mean that no matter how great we may think we are, none of us are islands. We have all been blessed, influenced, and inspired by the gifts of someone else. No one by themselves is the total package but together, by the connectivity of God's Holy Spirit, we can use our collective giftedness to impact our families, churches, and communities.

It Is All About Trust

Minister Jeannette Myers-Gilbert, Assistant Pastor
Pastoral Care, Zion Baptist Church, Ardmore, PA

"Trust in the Lord with all thine heart; and lean not unto thine own understanding…He shall direct thy paths."
Proverbs 3: 5-6 KJV

There he sat on the fourth step of the stairs leading up to the second floor, rocking and laughing, clapping his hands and laughing with sweet sounds of infectious joy as only a three year old could! My nephew sat laughing and rocking on that step as his father called to the adults to "Come and see; come on y'all, see what D. J.'s going to do!"

As we adults gathered around my brother-in-law at the bottom of the steps, he told D.J. to go up another step. Obediently, the little fellow planted both feet on the step and with both hands and feet working in concert with each other pushed his little bottom up another step. All the time laughing and laughing as if he and his Dad had a wonderful secret they were going to share with us adults pushing and bumping each other at the bottom of the steps in order to see what was going on.

41

With us adults trying to position ourselves to see, D.J., Dad told D.J. to stand up. Without hesitation, D.J. stood up, held his little arms out towards his Dad and with his little hands waving back and forth towards his Dad, his little body rocked in joyful anticipation as his father stretched out his arms to him, and shouted, "Jump." There was a loud gasp as all of us adults watched young three year old D.J. jump, laughing as he flew through the air into the waiting arms of his father.

I know you know where I am going with this story. It is knowing that when I go to God as a little child who does not need to figure things but just knows that His outstretched arms will catch me when I fall, that He will wipe away my tears when I cry, and give me words of encouragement when no one else will - that It **is** all about trust.

Trust, for us who know when we "lean not to our own understanding," our loving Father will "keep you from falling..." (Jude 24 KJV) and will "direct [our] thy paths." (Proverbs 3:6)

My Prayer: Father God, thank you for always being there for me.

Obedience is Better than Sacrifice

Rev. Albert G. Davis, Jr., Pastor
Mt. Calvary Baptist Church, Ardmore, PA

"How can I repay the Lord for all his goodness to me? I will lift up the cup of salvation and call on the name of the Lord. I will fulfill my vows to the Lord in the presence of all his people."
Psalm 116:12-14 (NIV)

And so, it is another day. And if I could honestly say, without fear of recrimination, without fear of people making more of it than the words actually say, without all of the "oohs, ahs and ohs," I would say, "I am tired."

But when I think of the Lord's goodness toward me – my life, my travels, my reputation, opening doors I didn't know existed, my family, my relationship with the Lord, even my mistakes and poor decisions -- something supersedes and overtakes the fatigue. Yes, I'm still tired, but a new motivation kicks in…a second wind, if you will.

How can I repay the Lord? Not with money or sacrifice; I will lift up the cup of salvation and call on the name of the Lord. I will look to the hills recognizing that my help comes from the Lord who made heaven and earth. I will fulfill (with joy) my vows to the Lord in the presence of all his people.

Father God, thank you for second winds. Thank you for moments of meditation that allows us to honestly confide in you where we are at any given moment. Thank you that even while we admit what we are presently feeling, we are always pointing and pointed towards … nevertheless, not my will but thy will be done.

The Gift of Eternal Life

Rev. April Martin, Pastor
Mt. Zion A.M.E, Devon, PA

"For the wages of sin is death; but the gift of God is eternal life through Jesus Christ our Lord." Romans 6:23

There are many different kinds of gifts and many different categories of gifts. A gift is something given voluntarily without payment in return. For instance things like furniture, jewelry like diamonds, clothes and cars just to name a few. With each gift or category of gift comes a description which tells the buyer or the giver exactly what kind of gift it is and what that particular gift is to be used for.

It does not matter how much each gift cost; it does not matter if thousands upon thousands of dollars are spent; most gifts at some point lose their value or worth and depreciate as time goes on.

The older the gift the more we tend to forget about it and the emotion that came along with receiving that particular gift. Earthly gifts can lose their usefulness or become outdated just as old technology such as computers and flip top phones.

But when we think of God and the gift that He has given us in Jesus Christ, we must begin to think on an entirely different realm.

First let's consider God our Father. As God he is incapable of giving anything that is not good. The Bible in James 1:17 reads, "Every good gift and every perfect gift is from above, and cometh down from the Father of lights, with whom there is no variableness, neither shadow of turning." He is our Father and from the foundation of the world intended to give us a gift of eternal value in His Son Jesus Christ.

Our challenge is to try and describe the indescribable. I just looked at my face book account and saw the following:

"The Greatest Man in History"

Jesus had no servants,
Yet they call Him Master
Had no degree,
But they called Him teacher
Had no medicines,
But they called Him Healer
He had no army,
Yet kings feared Him
He won no military battles,
But he conquered the world

He committed no crime,
But they crucified Him
He was buried in a tomb,
Yet He lives today.

(no author given)

To personalize this, I describe Jesus as just what I needed. For without the gift of Jesus there would be no opportunity to have the gift of eternal life. Romans 6:23 reads, "For the wages of sin is death; but the gift of God is eternal life through Jesus Christ our Lord."

One of the problems today is that people don't understand that we are eternal creatures made to live forever. That's one of the characteristics of God that was breathed on us in the garden. Therefore, we will spend eternity somewhere and because of God's gift of Jesus Christ we can spend eternity in His presence.

Until I go on to see just how long eternity is I must first go through this life. So I'm so glad that because of Jesus willing to go back to the Father, I now have the gift of the Holy Ghost. Acts 2:38 reads, "Then Peter said unto them, Repent, and be baptized every one of you in the name of Jesus Christ for the remission of sins, and ye shall receive the gift of the Holy Ghost." Because I gladly received Jesus as a gift from God I also receive the gift of the Holy

Ghost which enables me to live a more abundant and fruitful life while on this side of the Jordan.

Jesus, the gift of God that is so BEYOND human description until it takes a multitude of other gifts that flow from him to try and come close to a description worthy of who He is.

He will never lose his worth or value. And rather than lose value with time, the longer I have Him the more I appreciate and love who I have been given.

An Encounter with Jesus

Rev. Albert Johnson, Pastor
Tabor AME Church Philadelphia, PA

"Come; see a man who told me everything I ever did. Could this be the Messiah?" John 4:29 (read John 4:27-42)

One of the most demoralizing things in life is when you are stigmatized and ostracized because of who you are or are not. Additionally, not only is one placed in a category that can be demeaning but you are also told what you can and cannot have or achieve. Someone other than yourself is making a determination of your value and, your self-worth and entitlements based upon their prejudices, bigotry, and ignorance solely because of who you are, the mistakes you may have made, your economic status and education, to name just a few. This, being stigmatized, can lead to isolation, low self-esteem and a growing sense of nobodyness.

This is the challenge and circumstance faced by the Samaritan woman whom Jesus met at Jacob's well. This sister was an outcast of society due to her race and her less than desirable lifestyle. She had a promiscuous past and was of a despised race of people. Due to these circumstances, hers was not a pleasant life.

Our dear sister's life is not unlike many of our lives today. Many of us are constantly being tormented and punished for the mistakes of the past, by our lifestyle choices, gender, economic status, educational attainment (or lack thereof) or our race. And, like the Samaritan woman, we begin to accept this unacceptable treatment from others as the way it is supposed to be. Additionally, we allow other others to place limits on what we can achieve and what we can expect from life.

However, the good news is that your life can be forever changed, sins forgiven and your expectations raised after an encounter with Jesus.

After her encounter with Jesus, our Samaritan sister had renewed pride and greater sense of worth. She no longer hid in isolation ashamed by the mistakes of the past but went into town and declared "Come, see a man who told me everything I ever did. Could this be the Christ?"

Jesus had given her a gift of pride and enthusiasm for life that had been eroded. Because of the gift Jesus had given her, she now knew that her current condition did not have to be her conclusion. And, she realized that she could not keep it to herself but had to tell others about him. Many did not believe because of her testimony but after their own encounter with Jesus, they believed after hearing him for themselves.

My beloved, after an encounter with Jesus you will never be the same. Like our dear Samaritan sister, you must:

- Change who you are
- Tell somebody about the goodness of the Lord
- Invite Jesus into your life
- Get to know him for yourself

The Weaving of Our Lives Together

Rev. Dr. Marsha Brown Woodard
Saints Memorial Baptist Church, Bryn Mawr, PA

Woven together our journeys make us stronger for we are sisters and brothers made in the image of God.

God weaves us together in many ways and on many levels. God takes our individual journeys and weaves them together to become a congregation. Then God takes the journey of multiple congregations and weaves them together to become a community. And of course God then takes the journey of communities and weaves those together to create nations. God weaves them all together for the good.

But sometimes we resist the weaving, because growing as sisters and brothers in Christ is not always easy. Community takes work, but I believe the journey to community is worth every step that it takes.

Community is God's gift to us. It is in community that we learn to share our joys and catch one another's tears. It is in community that we learn to trust one another.
It is in community that we learn that to really listen to another sometimes takes courage, for we have to let go of

our assumptions and allow the other person to be who they really are.

Community takes hard work but it is worth the work. For it is in community that we really discover who we really are. In community we learn that we belong to God and that we are God's royal daughters and God's royal sons, who have been created for good. It is in community that we learn we are sisters and brothers made in the image of God and we learn to grow as the body of Christ

In community God can weave us together in ways that enable us to be a community of sisters and brothers who are willing to stand on our faith and to take risk for the kingdom. A community learning to value people more than things, relationships more than regulations and growing to be more loving as it grows to be more courageous.

Community will only happen as we are willing to let go of a 'we/they' mentality and to develop an 'us' mentality. Community will only happen as we are willing to stay at the table and work through our differences. Community will only happen when we seek to understand that we are but one body in Christ.

Community will happen as we remember that we have been made better through the love that Christ showed in laying down his life for us.

God is weaving us together so that we can turn the world upside down!

Translations Used In This Volume

- New International Version (NIV)
- Message Bible
- King James Version (KJV)
- Amplified Bible (AB)
- New Living Translation (NLT)
- New King James Version (NKJV)
- New Revised Standard Version (NRSV)
- New American Standard (NAS)

Do Not Forget the Assembling of the Saints

We invite you to worship with an Alliance Congregation

- **Bethel AME Ardmore** 163 Sheldon Lane Ardmore, PA 19003 *Rev. Carolyn Cavaness, Pastor*

- **Mt. Calvary Baptist**, 127 Walnut Avenue, Ardmore, PA 19003, *Rev. Albert G. Davis, Jr. Pastor*

- **Zion Baptist** Greenfield and West Spring Avenues, Ardmore, PA 19003 *Rev. Dr. James Pollard, Sr., Pastor*

- **Memorial Church of God In Christ**, 747 Buck Lane, Haverford, PA 19041, *Elder Darren Miller, Pastor*

- **Bethel A.M.E.** Bryn Mawr, 50 South Merion Avenue, Bryn Mawr, PA 19010, *Rev. Carlos Bounds, Pastor*

- **Saints Memorial Baptist**, 47 S. Warner Ave. Bryn Mawr, PA 19010 *Rev. Michael Stitt, Pastor*

- **First Baptist**, 1012 Upper Gulph Road, Wayne, PA 19087, *Rev. Rashad Groves, Pastor.*

- **St. John A.M.E**. 203 Highland Ave. Wayne, PA 19087, *Rev. Joell D. McDuffy, Pastor*

- **Second Baptist** 246 Highland Ave. Wayne, PA 19087, *Rev. Dr. Raymond Thomas, Pastor*

- **Mt. Zion A.M.E.** 380 North Fairfield Road, Devon, PA 19333, *Rev. April Martin, Pastor*

- **New Hope Baptist** Central Junction and Rt.30, Paoli, PA 19301, *Rev. Darrell Brown, Jr. Pastor*

- **St. Paul A.M.E.** 2nd and Church Street, Malvern, PA 19355,   *Rev. Hollis Howland, Pastor*

- **Greater Faith Baptist**, Malvern, PA 19355, *Rev. Delonte Reeves, Pastor*

www.ingramcontent.com/pod-product-compliance
Lightning Source LLC
Chambersburg PA
CBHW071850020426
42331CB00007B/1934